Beam of Light

The Story of the First White House Menorah

written by
Elisa Boxer

illustrated by
Sofia Moore

Rocky Pond Books

For Evan, my beam of light—E.B.

For my family—S.M.

ROCKY POND BOOKS
An imprint of Penguin Random House LLC, New York

First published in the United States of America by Rocky Pond Books,
an imprint of Penguin Random House LLC, 2024

Text copyright © 2024 by Elisa Boxer
Illustrations copyright © 2024 by Sofia Moore

Visit us online at PenguinRandomHouse.com.

Library of Congress Cataloging-in-Publication Data is available.

ISBN 9780593698174

1 3 5 7 9 10 8 6 4 2

Manufactured in China • TOPL

Design by Cerise Steel • Text set in Cream

The art was created using a mix of digital and traditional tools.

I was supposed to be destroyed.

The year was 1948, and I was part of a building on the brink of collapse.

The foundation was sinking.
The walls were crumbling.
The second-story floors had rotted so badly that a piano leg crashed through, poking down from the ceiling of the dining room below.

A report called for the residents to "evacuate the building at once."

But the man who lived there with his family didn't want to leave.

After all, this wasn't just any house.

This was The White House. The People's House.

The man was Harry S. Truman, President of the United States.

And I was a witness to the weakening—a wooden beam, struggling to support this structure that once stood strong.

But everything around me was crumbling.

Just five years earlier, I was witness to a deeper level of destruction.

In 1943, hundreds of rabbis walked up the White House steps. Some were crying. Some were praying. All were asking President Franklin Roosevelt for help. The Nazis were rounding up Jewish people in Eastern Europe, and these rabbis wanted the United States to offer them a safe haven.

But President Roosevelt turned them away.
Unwelcomed in the People's House.
Locked out of the land of the free.

By the time the next president, Harry S. Truman, took office two years later, six million Jewish people had been killed in the Holocaust.

The weight was almost too much to bear.

I was supposed to be destroyed.

A confidential memo called the building's breakdown "a matter of national concern."

Finally, President Truman agreed that the time had come to stop patching the problems and start creating a new home that would be stronger and safer for future generations.

Construction crews moved in.

The first family moved out.

And demolition began on a multi-million-dollar project to tear down and rebuild the inside of the White House.

Everything around me was reduced to rubble.

Bulldozers barreled through. Workers with wheelbarrows hauled away heaps of plaster and pipes, metal and marble, wires and wood.

I was supposed to be destroyed.

But I was spared. Salvaged.
Sent to a storage warehouse.

And there I sat, through thirteen presidents.
I was afraid I'd been forgotten.
But I come from strong roots.

In 2022, seventy years after construction workers carted me off to storage, carpenters opened the warehouse doors and let in the light.

They loaded me onto a truck and brought me to the basement of a house with tools that would transform me.

This wasn't just any house.

This was The White House. The People's House.

I had come home.

I was supposed to be destroyed.

Instead, master woodworkers made me
into a menorah. I held nine silver cups
that held nine glowing candles

that held the centuries-old story of a small band
of Jewish underdogs who defended their freedom
against a huge army of Persian persecutors.

In a special Chanukah ceremony, in this house once on the verge of collapse, surrounded by rabbis and Holocaust survivors and their children and their children's children, President Joseph Biden introduced me as the first Jewish artifact ever added to the White House's permanent collection.

I can never be removed.

In past years, presidents lit borrowed menorahs,
on loan from various families and temples.

They were always temporary.

"This year," President Biden said, "we thought it was important to celebrate Chanukah with another message of significance: Permanence."

I am the foundation of that permanence.

I am the centerpiece of the story of the oil that lasted longer than anyone expected.

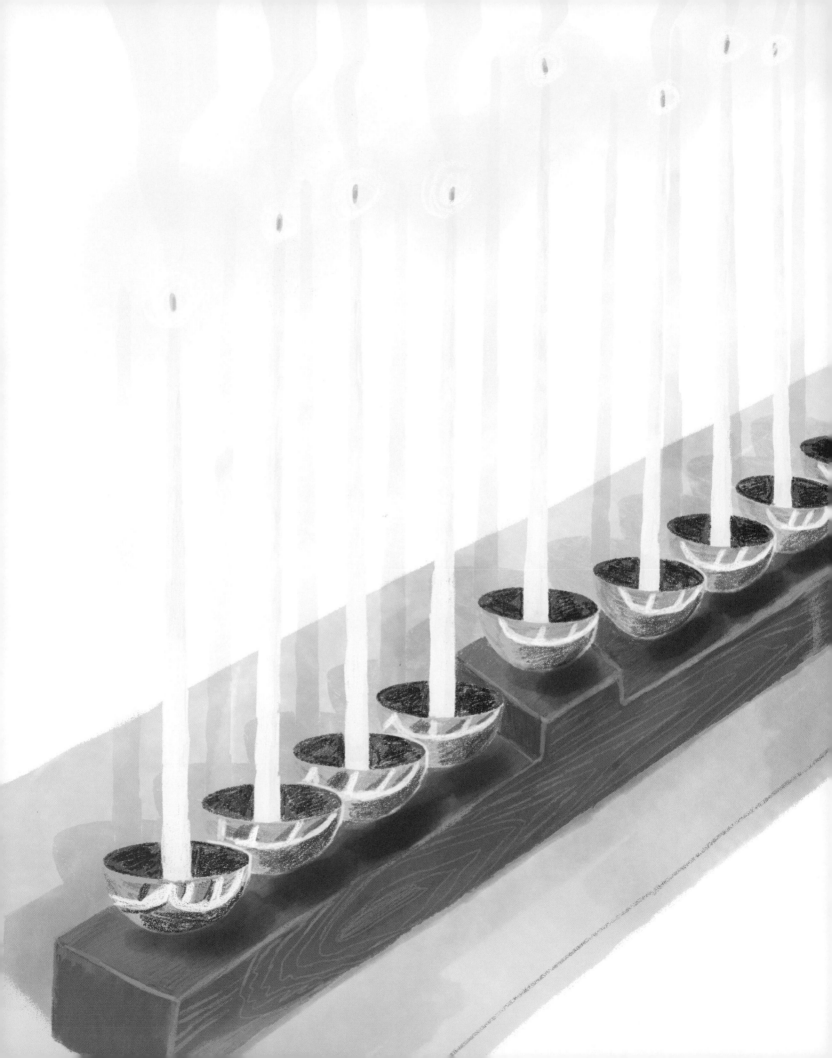

I was supposed to be destroyed.

Instead, I became a beam of light,
a reminder of the miracle,
a symbol of strength for
generations to come.

Author's Note

On December 19, 2022, President Joseph Biden welcomed guests for a Chanukah celebration, and this menorah made history at the White House.

Created from a piece of reclaimed wood salvaged during the Truman-era renovation, it was the first piece of Judaica ever to be added to the White House Holiday Collection. Menorahs lit by past presidents had always been temporary—loaned from private collections or synagogues.

In 2001, for example, President George W. Bush lit a menorah made in Ukraine and loaned to the White House by New York's Jewish Museum. He was actually the first president to light a menorah in the White House. In 2010, President Barack Obama lit a menorah that had been saved from a Louisiana synagogue damaged by Hurricane Katrina, but it went back to the synagogue after the White House celebration.

Once an item becomes part of the official White House Holiday Collection, it is considered a permanent fixture of the archives, and can't be removed by any future administration.

It was a significant time for the debut of a permanent piece of Judaica, as the number of anti-Semitic incidents targeting Jewish Americans reached an all-time high during the previous year, according to the Anti-Defamation League. As the menorah was installed in its new home, the blessing over the candles was chanted by Rabbi Charlie Cytron-Walker, who, earlier that same year, had managed to free himself and his congregants from hostage takers at his synagogue in Texas.

When I learned that this menorah was made from an old beam salvaged when the Truman White House was gutted, I was struck by the symbolism of renewal and survival; the parallels of this wooden beam to the resilience of the Jewish people, and the idea for this book was born.

The Truman-era demolition and renovation came just a few years after the Rabbis March on Washington, when four hundred rabbis from around the country marched up the White House steps with a petition and a request to meet with President Theodore Roosevelt. They were looking to draw attention to the atrocities being committed in Eastern Europe, and seeking refuge for the Jewish people being killed by the Nazis. But President Roosevelt turned them away, and six million Jewish people ended up being killed in the Holocaust.

Some of the old building materials from the Truman-era demolition went to landfills, some were repurposed in the reconstruction phase, and others, like this wooden beam, were put into storage. The idea of wood coming from strong roots, withstanding time, and realizing that what appears to be destruction could in fact be transformation, was on my mind as I wrote this story.

The story of Chanukah itself is also one of reclamation and rebirth—a celebration of Judah Maccabee and his underdog band of followers defending their religious freedom and overcoming oppression to reclaim the holy temple in Jerusalem against all odds. The oil in that menorah that was only enough to last for one night, instead burned for eight.

When things feel hard and the odds feel insurmountable and the world feels dark, may you recall this wooden beam and its journey. And may you too remember that you came here to hold the light.

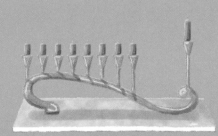

Selected Bibliography

Cook, Nancy, Jordan Fabian, and Akayla Gardner. "Biden condemns 'violent venom' of antisemitism at Hanukkah event." *Bloomberg News*, December 19, 2022.

Engelhard, Jack. "The Rabbis March on Washington, 1943." *Israel National News*, April 24, 2017.

Furman, Bess. "White House is Closing as Unsafe." *The New York Times,* November 7, 1948.

Hayashi-Smith, Donna. "Lighting the Menorah: Celebrating Hanukkah at the White House." The White House Historical Association, November 23, 2020.

Kurtz, Judy. "New White House Menorah Makes History." *The Hill*, December 15, 2022.

"Mr. Truman's Renovation: Demolition." The White House Historical Association.

Nilsson, Jeff. "Destroying and Saving the White House." *The Saturday Evening Post*, February 16, 2011.

Treisman, Rachel. "As the Bidens mark Hanukkah, the White House gets its own menorah for the first time." *NPR*, December 19, 2022.

"When the White House Had to be Completely Gutted, 1949–1952." Rare Historical Photos, December 11, 2021.